The Dwarf Planets

by Betsy Rathburn
Illustrated by Natalya

BLASTOFF!
MISSIONS

BELLWETHER MEDIA
MINNEAPOLIS, MN

Blastoff! Missions takes you on a learning adventure! Colorful illustrations and exciting narratives highlight cool facts about our world and beyond. Read the mission goals and follow the narrative to gain knowledge, build reading skills, and have fun!

BLASTOFF!
MISSIONS

Traditional Nonfiction

BLASTOFF! READERS

BLASTOFF! Beginners

BLASTOFF! DISCOVERY

BLASTOFF! MISSIONS

Narrative Nonfiction

Blastoff! Universe

MISSION GOALS

> FIND YOUR SIGHT WORDS IN THE BOOK.

> LEARN ABOUT THE DIFFERENT DWARF PLANETS IN OUR SOLAR SYSTEM.

> CHOOSE A DWARF PLANET THAT YOU WOULD LIKE TO LEARN MORE ABOUT.

This edition first published in 2023 by Bellwether Media, Inc.

No part of this publication may be reproduced in whole or in part without written permission of the publisher. For information regarding permission, write to Bellwether Media, Inc., Attention: Permissions Department, 6012 Blue Circle Drive, Minnetonka, MN 55343.

Library of Congress Cataloging-in-Publication Data

Names: Rathburn, Betsy, author.
Title: The dwarf planets / by Betsy Rathburn.
Description: Minneapolis, MN : Bellwether Media, 2023. | Series: Blastoff! missions. Journey into space | Includes bibliographical references and index. | Audience: Ages 5-8 | Audience: Grades 2-3 |
Summary: "Vibrant illustrations accompany information about the dwarf planets in the solar system. The narrative nonfiction text is intended for students in kindergarten through third grade" Provided by publisher.
Identifiers: LCCN 2022006868 (print) | LCCN 2022006869 (ebook) | ISBN 9781644876541 (library binding) | ISBN 9781648348389 (paperback) | ISBN 9781648347009 (ebook)
Subjects: LCSH: Dwarf planets--Juvenile literature. | Asteroid belt--Juvenile literature. | Kuiper Belt--Juvenile literature.
Classification: LCC QB698 .R38 2023 (print) | LCC QB698 (ebook) | DDC 523.4--dc23/eng20220422
LC record available at https://lccn.loc.gov/2022006868
LC ebook record available at https://lccn.loc.gov/2022006869

Editor: Derek Zobel   Designer: Jeffrey Kollock

Printed in the United States of America, North Mankato, MN.

This is **Blastoff Jimmy**! He is here to help you on your mission and share fun facts along the way!

Table of Contents

Small Worlds

Cool!

You get home from school. There is a new book on your desk. It is about the dwarf planets in our **solar system**! You imagine visiting these small, faraway worlds. Time for a space journey!

In the Asteroid Belt

Ceres

You weave through lumpy rocks in the **asteroid belt**. Soon, you spot Ceres. It is the smallest dwarf planet. But it is the asteroid belt's largest object!

asteroids

You try to count
its many **craters**.
Some look white.
Could that be water?

You lean in for a
closer look. But Ceres
keeps spinning.
Time to move on!

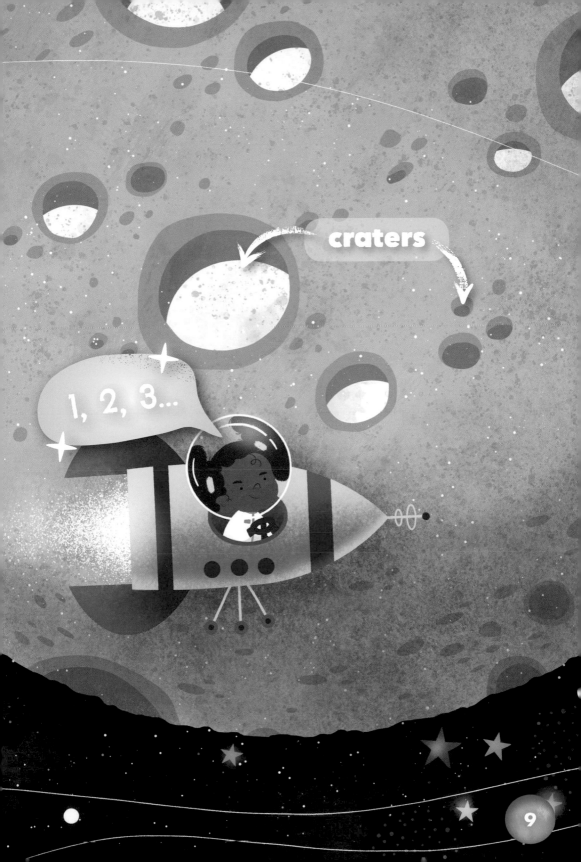

In the Kuiper Belt

Kuiper Belt

The journey to the **Kuiper Belt** is long. Pluto is your next stop. Flying close, you notice that the dwarf planet is spinning on its side!

Pluto

You peer down at Pluto's light surface. Mountains cover it. What would they be like to climb?

Charon

In the distance, you spot Pluto's biggest moon. Charon is almost half Pluto's size!

Haumea

Oval-shaped Haumea catches your eye next. It looks like a big, gray egg. It spins fast!

ring

You look closely to see Haumea's thin **ring**. Beyond, two small moons **orbit**.

You turn from Haumea and head toward the edge of the solar system. Makemake looks mysterious. What lies on its red surface?

► **JIMMY SAYS** ◄

It takes Makemake over 300 times longer than Earth to orbit the Sun!

Makemake

You spot a dim object orbiting Makemake. Could that be a moon?

Eris

Eris is your last stop. It looks cold and rocky. Far off, you spot Eris's moon in orbit.

The Sun is even farther away. It looks like a tiny dot.

Suddenly, you are drawn away from Eris. You look up from your book. Your dad is calling you for dinner. Welcome home from your dwarf planet adventure!

The Dwarf Planets

Ceres

How to say it: SEER-ees

Dwarf Planet Size Rank: 5

Moons: 0

Pluto

How to say it: PLOO-tow

Dwarf Planet Size Rank: 1

Moons: 5

Haumea

How to say it: HA-may-uh

Dwarf Planet Size Rank: 3

Moons: 2

Makemake

How to say it: MAH-kay-MAH-kay

Dwarf Planet Size Rank: 4

Moons: maybe 1

Eris

How to say it: eh-RIS

Dwarf Planet Size Rank: 2

Moons: 1

Glossary

asteroid belt–a part of the solar system between Mars and Jupiter where more than one million asteroids are found

craters–holes in the surface of an object

Kuiper Belt–a part of the solar system beyond Neptune where many small objects orbit

orbit–to move in a fixed path around something

ring–a band of small objects such as rocks and ice that circles around a planet

solar system–the group of planets, moons, asteroids, and other bodies that circle around the Sun

To Learn More

AT THE LIBRARY

Leaf, Christina. *The Outer Planets*. Minneapolis, Minn.: Bellwether Media, 2023.

Ringstad, Arnold. *Dwarf Planets*. Mankato, Minn.: The Child's World, 2020.

Scott, Elaine. *To Pluto and Beyond: The Amazing Voyage of New Horizons*. New York, N.Y.: Viking, 2018.

ON THE WEB

FACTSURFER

Factsurfer.com gives you a safe, fun way to find more information.

1. Go to www.factsurfer.com.

2. Enter "dwarf planets" into the search box and click 🔍.

3. Select your book cover to see a list of related content.

BEYOND THE MISSION

> WHICH DWARF PLANET IS YOUR FAVORITE? WHY?

> DRAW YOUR OWN DWARF PLANET. WHAT DOES IT LOOK LIKE? WHERE IS IT?

> DO YOU THINK CERES'S CRATERS HAVE WATER? WHY OR WHY NOT?

Index